WHY 75% OF PODCASTS FAIL AND HOW YOU CAN AVOID IT

WHAT 100+ PODCASTERS WISH THEY KNEW BEFORE STARTING PODCASTING, KEY GROWTH HACKS FOR BEGINNERS

DANIEL LARSON

AT PUBLISHING

CONTENTS

INTRODUCTION

Podcasting is an exciting new medium that has exploded in popularity over the past few years. It's easy to get started, but even easier to fall into the 75% of podcasts that cease to exist. **Yep, you heard that right.** From 90 days to 12 months, 132,000 of the total 540,000 created a new show in all of 2017. This means under 25% of all podcasts have a new production. Consequently; 75% of podcasts are no longer in production. This stat is a little old...but a more recent update shows that things haven't gotten much better. An article on www.9to5mac.com references data from Apple Podcasts, Podcast Index and Amplifi Media to show that although there are close to 2.5 million shows (April 2021), a shocking 44% don't make it past their third episode. And the number of podcasts with 10 or more episodes? Around 720k.

Podcasting is the new blogging. Or at least that's what everyone says. But how do you know if podcasting is right for you? Do you have a message to share with the world? Are you ready to put in the work to grow your audience? Podcasts are an excellent way of reaching people all over the world, and they're easier than ever to create thanks to cheaper equipment and software. If this sounds like something that might interest you, then read on!

I have been a podcasting author for almost 2 years now (gosh, time flies when you're having fun). Besides having 2 Amazon bestsellers to my name, most of my knowledge and expertise comes from helping my students go from confused and doubtful to clear and confident on how to optimize their show for growth, and take their podcast to new heights. One even managed to get into the top 0.5% of shows globally! Don't get me wrong though, I'm not taking the credit - he had an amazing show, but just needed some clarity and direction. In addition, I've spoken to well over a thousand podcasters in the incredibly welcoming and supportive podcasting Facebook community, which I feel privileged to be a part of. If you're not all that involved in this kind of stuff, I recommend you start by joining some of the more active communities. Mine is called *Podcast Marketing Made Simple* and we hold weekly live calls, provide daily tips, thought-provoking questions and have regular discussions on everything podcasting related. It probably goes without saying that all the podcasters who kindly gave their insights to you as a reader of this book are also part of the community. Don't miss out!

You won't find another resource like this one anywhere else on the internet - it's truly unique! Don't waste any more time wondering - get it all straight from the horse's mouth. In fact, a triple-digit sum of mouths. It's not as intimidating or gross as it might sound, I promise.

Over one hundred amazing podcasters contributed to this book with their insights and wisdom. The special thing is, collectively they cover the entire podcasting demographic. All ages, all continents, all types of shows. Some have been podcasting for less than 3 months, some for over 10 years! What's fascinating is that upon reading through all their main takeaways from podcasting and trying to maintain and grow their shows, you start to see many common trends, both in hurdles faced and valuable revelations. Even some genius hacks have popped up more than once. With each podcaster's log is their show name and a brief sentence about their show, so you can go and check a podcast out as you wish. (To give the 'time as a podcaster' stat a point of reference, the questions were answered by podcasters through October & November 2021)

We all have 24 hours in a day, but how we choose to spend them can make or break our success as podcasters. With this guide, you won't waste any more of your valuable time on things that aren't helping your show grow! You'll learn how to make the same progress but with less of the time and money-wasting mistakes. Of course, it must be noted that some mistakes are necessary to actually make first-hand, because of the lessons we learn as a result. They must be learned 'the hard way'. Put alternatively, *there are no shortcuts to success.* This book won't shield you from the necessary learning curve - that's just part of the process, and a process you will love. What it will do is get rid of the unnecessary mistakes most make, which comfortably outnumber the mandatory 'life lessons' of podcasting.

Bottom line is, reading this book will save you time and money. Not to undermine the importance of saving your energy for the things that truly matter most...which you will identify in this book.

Let's see what everyone has to share.

Daniel Larson

Name: Big Lou

Time as a podcaster: 18 months

Show: Go Produce

'We help committed indie music artists and their communities profit off of their passion.'

What do you wish you knew before starting podcasting?

Keep it simple to start. This is a whole world of new. Please understand that. For all that you think you know there is still more to learn and that is said for anyone at any level of knowledge. Process patiently but also with no fear. Ask questions and risk appearing foolish because the reward is gained knowledge. The more you can learn the more efficient than you can become. If you can make this an efficient process you are A LOT more likely to enjoy it in its entirety. It will get challenging so keep your goal in mind.

What's the biggest hack you've learned that you wish you could tell your younger podcasting self?

Riverside.fm is the answer. I tried making Zoom work because we were trying to incorporate extra elements into the podcast to make it more visually exciting but it over complicated matters. Riverside.fm has solutions to lots of problems and still allows you the freedom to make certain creative edits. It also helped us operate remotely which is huge!

Name: Tristan Abbott

Time as a podcaster: September 2020

Show: The Wolf AND The Shepherd

'The only show to defy all expectations. By having none.'

What do you wish you knew before starting podcasting?

Probably how easy it was to start otherwise we would have started at least a year previously. Although we have approx. 120 podcasts under our belt, there was a delay of close to a year before we started because it just seemed to daunting of a task to get going but the set up from idea to release is so easy that at the basic level, all you need is a laptop with a microphone and you're good to go.

What's the biggest hack you've learned that you wish you could tell your younger podcasting self?

Don't waste hours on pre-production scripts for guests that you never use anyway. We found it more natural and flowing to abolish scripts past the intro/outro and we almost always have feedback on how laid back and fun our podcast is.

Name: Stephanie

Time as a podcaster: 10 months

Show: The Historia Podcast

'Travelling through history, one episode at a time.'

What do you wish you knew before starting podcasting?

Before I even got into podcasting it took a lot of time finding the equipment and an editing software that could meet my needs. I spent a lot of time trying to learn how to edit audio as well, but once you've done that, there's an even bigger task. Depending on your topic, there's a lot of research and sometimes money that goes into just prepping for an episode and even though it's been a few months, I've sometimes struggled finding a system that could help me balance everything.

What's the biggest hack you've learned that you wish you could tell your younger podcasting self?

Breath. You aren't failing because you feel overwhelmed.

Name: Antionette Blake

Time as a podcaster: Started in 2017

Show: Out & About with Antionette

'Interviewing people who are making it happen!'

What do you wish you knew before starting podcasting?

I started my first show, "Social Media Sunday with the Delaware Blogger" in 2017, and it was a live call in show with interviews. I wish that I would have pre-recorded the shows so that I could have vetted some of the callers. Although, there was only a few episodes in which callers wanted nothing more than to promote themselves or their projects nor were they really interested in bringing value to the conversation or the topic. Thankfully, there were not major disasters.

I also wished that I had kept or downloaded copies of the MP3s because shortly after I left the production company, they closed the account with the hosting company, Blog Talk Radio and didn't transfers any of my shows to their new platform so I lost all of my episodes which totaled more than 150 and now all the links are broken in my blog posts that featured and promoted those shows.

What's the biggest hack you've learned that you wish you could tell your younger podcasting self?

Blankets, comforters or moving blankets attached to the walls make perfect "acoustic tiles" and are cheaper too!

Name: Phteve (pronounced "Fteve")

Time as a podcaster: Just a little over a year.

Show: One Outta One

'Popping bubbles in Jesus' name.

What do you wish you knew before starting podcasting?

I wish I had understood how much work it was going to be. Even just doing a 15 minute episode every week can be very taxing. If you don't prepare, Your content will be garbage. If your content is garbage, you won't have an audience. Therefore you need to take time to understand what your goal is, what the message is, and how you're going to deliver it (comedy, talk show with guests, newscast). If you don't take the time to prepare these things especially your goal and message, you will not be successful. Even then there's a chance it may not go anywhere and we need to all be OK with that possibility.

What's the biggest hack you've learned that you wish you could tell your younger podcasting self?

Always have a guest! OK maybe not always, but having guests, even if they are your friend from down the road, is always helpful. My best episodes are the ones I've done with my childhood buddy. I'm funnier, he brings something to the table I don't, and it's just more enjoyable to listen to two people talk instead of one.

Name: Dr. Karen M. Bryson

Time as a podcaster: Eight months

Show: The Curious Professor

'A podcast for the curious at heart. Be curious with Dr. B.'

What do you wish you knew before starting podcasting?

The main thing I wish I understood before I started podcasting was the importance of selecting a targeted niche. With the number of podcasts available online, it's much easier to gain momentum if you can appeal to a very targeted audience. It's been much more difficult for me to develop a fanbase because the topic of my show is broad rather than specialized.

🎙

What's the biggest hack you've learned that you wish you could tell your younger podcasting self?

Unless you have a live show, it's okay to make mistakes because it can be edited out. I was so worried about things being "perfect" when I interviewed guests that I missed opportunities to have a more authentic conversation. As I have become more comfortable as a podcaster, and more skilled at interviewing people, I have allowed conversations to flow more naturally and let go of the need for it to be exactly as I planned. I would tell my younger self to relax and have more fun with it!

Name: William Morgan

Time as a podcaster: Over 10 years

Show: The Geek Gauntlet Podcast

'The fastest hour in podcasting'

What do you wish you knew before starting podcasting?

I wish I knew more about audio. I started using a headset mic for a very long time and knew nothing about audio. But now I know about microphones and sound boards and my audio has improved over the years.

What's the biggest hack you've learned that you wish you could tell your younger podcasting self?

Research.....Get to know the podcasting game from all sides of it.

Name: Mike Cavaggioni

Time as a podcaster: 1 year

Show: Average Joe Finances

'Financial freedom starts here. Beat debt, build your wealth, & control your future.'

What do you wish you knew before starting podcasting?

I wish I knew to promote my podcast before launching. This is one of the things I tell everyone I know that is preparing to start a podcast. It's perfectly ok to start hyping your show up and sharing small clips. The podcasters I've worked with that have done this had significantly more downloads than those who have not.

I also wish I knew that its ok to make mistakes and not try to be a perfectionist. I wasted so much time trying to ensure that every product I put out was perfect. Sure, it's important to make sure you put out a good product, but it is not worth the time or effort to ensure perfection.

What's the biggest hack you've learned that you wish you could tell your younger podcasting self?

The biggest hack I've learned is that if you want to monetize, you need to learn to prioritize. I had to learn to step outside of my comfort zone and give up some control, I started outsourcing certain aspects of the show. I don't edit my own podcast anymore; I hired an editing team. That small change helped me free up time and allowed for me to have a better product. This resulted in a significant increase in downloads, sponsorships, and increased revenue. The podcast is self-sufficient now and pays for itself. It's turned something that was a hobby into another source of income. I am making money doing something I really enjoy, and you can't beat that!

Name: Anthony Maletestinic

Time as a podcaster: A year and 8 months

Show: Shed Talk Podcast

'Shed Talk Podcast'

What do you wish you knew before starting podcasting?

The main thing I wish I knew before I started was to have a consistency in your podcast. What consistency involves is a topic that you can talk about with multiple subtopics so you can expand on the thoughts you have (like creating a season for a show.)

🎙️

What's the biggest hack you've learned that you wish you could tell your younger podcasting self?

Utilize the tools in front of you! There's many podcasting tools out on the internet such as Anchor that have allowed me to publish my podcast on larger platforms such as Apple Podcasts, Spotify, Google Podcasts, and many more!

Name: Ayomide Giwa

Time as a podcaster: 1 year

Show: Last Words with Babs

'Making impact through stories '

What do you wish you knew before starting podcasting?

I wish I knew how much work and consistency went into it, however I used as more of just another insight into my life and viewpoints that matter. I didn't know the amount of people that would tune into it, and the impact it would have. The more consistent and persistent you are, the faster your growth, as well as impact that you can make.

What's the biggest hack you've learned that you wish you could tell your younger podcasting self?

I wouldn't say I have a hack, but one thing that has served me well personally is mixing it up by having guests on. Reason being they share different perspectives to a topic and can open a discussion between my audience which helps me to learn continually as well.

Name: Raven Scott

Time as a podcaster: 1 year

Show: The Thriving Intuitive

'Keep Your Unique Light Shining'

What do you wish you knew before starting podcasting?

I wish I knew it wasn't just a post and they will come format... I wish I knew it was a full time business for it to grow and thrive. I wish I knew it wasn't another form of social marketing, but if it's to be successful, it needs to be quality, thought out, an experience, and marketed out to a warm audience.

What's the biggest hack you've learned that you wish you could tell your younger podcasting self?

Title is everything to catch them to listen. The hack I learned from the author is to search the podcast for the episodes topic, then search Google, and come up with an amazing title based on the results of those two searches. Brilliant!

Name: Chip Hazard

Time as a podcaster: 2 years

Show: Movement Radio

'The Podcast about everything!'

What do you wish you knew before starting podcasting?

The main thing I wish I knew before I started podcasting would be just to go for it, you will never be truly ready but you can learn along the way and get better. I learned by asking other people in the podcast industry and everyone I have learned from has been super helpful and easy to talk to.

What's the biggest hack you've learned that you wish you could tell your younger podcasting self?

I would say the biggest hack I have learned since I started podcasting would be to reuse older episode snippets to upload to social media to drum up listeners. I would also consider using Hootsuite to maintain and upload to all social media accounts at once.

Name: Caroline K Schafer

Time as a podcaster: 3.5 years

Show: Courageously Grateful

'Courageously Grateful is a mindset to help you realize the depth of your courage and find gratitude when you don't think you can.'

What do you wish you knew before starting podcasting?

It doesn't have to be perfect to start! You don't need fancy equipment and expensive software. If you love what you're doing, all of the other stuff will come eventually. And take the time to listen and learn to others. But whatever you do - don't lose sight of why you wanted to start a podcast to begin with. In the end, you are connecting with other people. That's what this is all about. You have a message and you believe it's important to share it. Also, schedule time in your personal life to record, edit, create your graphic and when you're going to put the episodes out. That was something I did for others, as a podcast producer/editor, but not for my own. Don't take your own podcast for granted.

What's the biggest hack you've learned that you wish you could tell your younger podcasting self?

Have confidence in your ability. Trust yourself. Believe in yourself and your message.

Name: Kai'Lea

Time as a podcaster: 16 months

Show: Boss Sitch Boss Chick Corner

'Discussing business, life and music the boss way!'

What do you wish you knew before starting podcasting?

I wish I would have had a more strategic plan on how to reach my target audience. I simply jumped in with the intention to help everyone. But the broader things were, the more difficult it seemed to feel out an audience.

🎤

What's the biggest hack you've learned that you wish you could tell your younger podcasting self?

I've learned to focus in on the things that I relate to and niche my target audience down. I am a music lover and artist. Music is derived off of emotions so it is only fair to discuss those topics that music is geared toward. As for my non profit, that is still something I need to work on and I will need the help of my co-host to niche down the target. When you are clear on who you are targeting, the topics become clearer and its easier to reach the people. It is going to take hard work. They aren't going to come to you so you must be strong enough to handle the late nights and lengthy conversations as well as the act of pitching your show time after time.

Name: Lance Peppler

Time as a podcaster: Around 2 years

Show: Lance Peppler

'The Business Bookshelf podcast'

What do you wish you knew before starting podcasting?

That it would bring so much joy and also frustration.

Interviewing authors from around the world is one of the highlights of the week and I learn so much from each interview.

The frustration is that when I started I thought that the download numbers would steadily grow and had a hope that it might even grow exponentially. I have tried every suggestion to market the podcast but the actual downloads have actually decreased rather than increased. There is hope though that the next idea will work or the next guest will cause the podcast to go "viral".

What's the biggest hack you've learned that you wish you could tell your younger podcasting self?

Have a routine. I have setup a routine that works for me - read the author's book, prepare the interview script, setup the interview, have the interview, edit the interview, release the episode and then promote it. If broken up into activities on different days then the entire process won't seem to be as long as it actually is.

Name: Jeff Dawson

Time as a podcaster: 1 year

Show: Dawson's Domain

'#DawsonsDomain'

What do you wish you knew before starting podcasting?

Lining up more guests and staying on topic.

What's the biggest hack you've learned that you wish you could tell your younger podcasting self?

Be prepared when you go live. Don't fumble through notes or websites. Take the time to be properly prepared. It's okay if you need to reference an article or two, but make sure you have them up and running so you don't have any dead air time. That is the death for any radio show. It's not television where people have visuals. All they have is your voice and if someone tune in and they don't hear you, they move on to the next show.

Name: EML Goeloe

Time as a podcaster: 7 months

Show: EML Goeloe

'Dream Believe achieve the podcast'

What do you wish you knew before starting podcasting?

It takes time and energy. The guilt of not being consistent

What's the biggest hack you've learned that you wish you could tell your younger podcasting self?

....

Name: Lourdes Gant

Time as a podcaster: 5 months

Show: The Business Of Aquaculture Podcast

This is the podcast for the sustainable business movement in the aquafarming and ocean ranching industries. This podcast aims to amplify the voices of entrepreneurs addressing the UN Global Goals aka Sustainable Development Goal - SDG14 - to conserve and sustainably use the oceans and the seas.'

What do you wish you knew before starting podcasting?

I wish I knew sooner how good for leverage this platform is in reaching out to experts in our industry.

🎙

What's the biggest hack you've learned that you wish you could tell your younger podcasting self?

Never underestimate the power of asking previous guests to refer new guests :)

Name: Michael Cooper

Time as a podcaster: 3 years

Show: Scoobi and Chooi Show

'The scoobi and chooi show'

What do you wish you knew before starting podcasting?

Wait to invest in podcasting until it invests in you because it could lead to burn out.

What's the biggest hack you've learned that you wish you could tell your younger podcasting self?

Just be who you are, someone is waiting for you to shine.

Name: John Ashton

Time as a podcaster: 7 years

Show: Those Weekend Golf Guys

'We Talk A Good Game'

What do you wish you knew before starting podcasting?

I wish I had understood the need to be familiar with multiple disciplines. Most of us come from a singular background. We did one thing for a living. With podcasting, unless you are willing to outsource many aspects, you need to learn to become a Jack-Of-All-Trades.

I came from a broadcasting background. when I needed a sponsor, I called the Sales dept. If we needed publicity, we called the promotions people. And when the mixer broke, we called the engineer. Podcasting is, for the most part, a solo journey. Now I am the engineer, salesman, promotions person, etc. It took me a while to learn those other talents. Podcasting is more than talking for a living.

Don't be intimidated by the technology. While you will be told that a microphone and a computer are all you need to create and maintain a podcast, sound quality will not necessarily attract listeners if it is high quality, but it will definitely cause listeners to tune out and never return if the sound quality is bad.

Editing is important. Make the podcast flow. If it is hard to listen to, people won't (listen).

♪

What's the biggest hack you've learned that you wish you could tell your younger podcasting self?

I was lucky in that I was taught this at an early stage of my career. When addressing your audience, refer to them in the singular. We are lucky in English. We have only one word for "you" and it is the same if we are addressing an individual or a group. we simply say, "you". Use the word "you" when addressing your audience; not "everybody" "Y'all" "gang" or any of those collective nouns. You want to create a relationship with your listeners and while you want that group of listeners to be as large as possible, the listener will be more apt to become a fan if they can feel a direct relationship to you. They don't want to be part of a group. They want to hear you talking directly to them. You can create that illusion by using the word "you". And bring them into the conversation by using that word.

"I am feeling a bit sad now that Summer is over. I'm sure "you" feel that way too, right?"

That type of verbiage will cause the listener to feel the conversation is more intimate, maybe directed at them individually. Once they feel that way, you have developed a personal relationship and now have a loyal fan.

And one more thing, if I might. Once you publish and have that first episode up you have put yourself "out there". People will like what you do. People will not like what you do. Both types will possibly make their feelings known to you thru reviews and feedback. Positive reviews bolster your ego, make you smile, get those juices flowing and make you eager to get the next episode finished. Negative reviews have just the opposite effect and can bring you down into the dumps of despair and question whether to continue or not.

Pay no attention to them! I adopted this idea early on and it helped me ignore the Negative Nellies and the Naysayers: DO NOT ACCEPT CRITICISM FROM ANYONE YOU WOULD NOT GO TO FOR ADVICE

Name: Katherine-Lucy Bates

Time as a podcaster: 8 months

Show: Growing Through Dance

'Dance to Live, Live to Dance'

What do you wish you knew before starting podcasting?

The amount of time it would take me to edit, I am very aware that I want the best quality of interview.

What's the biggest hack you've learned that you wish you could tell your younger podcasting self?

Ensure you tell all your guests to promote the podcast- they don't automatically - need to have a checklist for them, provide them with social media graphic and ensure it's on style for their business/brand.

Name: My Alien Life Podcast

Time as a podcaster: 1 year

Show: My Alien Life Podcast

'It's like NPR with aliens!!!'

What do you wish you knew before starting podcasting?

To start sooner. I was in radio and producing for decades. I was lazy and should have started in 2000...The knowledge was there and the desire wasn't....DO IT NOW!!

What's the biggest hack you've learned that you wish you could tell your younger podcasting self?

Keep old mobile phones. They integrate perfectly with the RODECaster Pro. You can have one mobile connected via bluetooth for incoming calls, one wired for incoming calls from a free Google phone number. OR you can use the phones for ZOOM, and

Skype and mobile connections at the same time. It blows your equipment up 100 FOLD...

Name: Sen Zhan

Time as a podcaster: 1.5 years

Show: Sen Zhan

'Beyond Asian: Stories of the Third Culture'

What do you wish you knew before starting podcasting?

It's better for your work to be published and imperfect, than for it to be perfect (in your mind), and take forever to publish, or not be published at all. Your work is there to serve an audience, and they will *not* care if there are too many breaths, an extra um here and there, or if your cuts might be a little abrupt. They care more that they can receive what you have to share. For you to be concerned with only publishing things that you consider 'perfect' enough serves more your own ego than the people you created your podcast for.

If you're wondering, it's good enough. Just publish. Your work will naturally get better the more you do it. And your idea of what is good may not actually be what your audience considers good enough. Just publish.

What's the biggest hack you've learned that you wish you could tell your younger podcasting self?

Not to make this a marketing thing, but starting to use Descript as an editing software cut down my production time massively because I could edit directly from the transcript.

Also, get feedback early and often. Ask for help. Try different formats. Do what feels fun, rather than what you think it's supposed to be.

Name: Craig McFarland

Time as a podcaster: Six years

Show: Beyond the Mouse

'All things Disney for NPR Illinois Community Voices'

What do you wish you knew before starting podcasting?

I wish I would have known how valuable it is to be confident in your own voice. You have your own unique perspective that you bring to this world. Use it! Just get into the game.

🎙

What's the biggest hack you've learned that you wish you could tell your younger podcasting self?

Honestly, smart links save so much time. People listen to your show from all over the place, on all sorts of platforms. There are lots of smart link places out there, our network uses link tree.

Name: Saadiah Angster

Time as a podcaster: 1.5 years

Show: Saadiah Angster

Jewish Boy Calls His Mother'

What do you wish you knew before starting podcasting?

I knew a lot based off of the Facebook groups and blogs that I read before. The only thing I can really tell is to be genuine and do the podcast for yourself.

What's the biggest hack you've learned that you wish you could tell your younger podcasting self?

Use Zoom and Headliner.

Name: Amelia Rose Zimlich

Time as a podcaster: A year and 5 months

Show: C'est La Me

'Love, life and authenticity'

What do you wish you knew before starting podcasting?

Before podcasting, I wish I knew how many resources there are for podcasters! Although I am not a professional podcaster, I wanted my show to do well, but was unaware of the various tools I had access to. From general software that comes in handy for any business to podcast-focused technology, there is a multitude of resources that can help podcasters with sound engineering, analytics measurement, statistics, audience connection, ad placement, podcasting questions - pretty much anything you need help with! Knowing about those tools before I started C'est La Me would have made me feel more equipped to begin podcasting.

What's the biggest hack you've learned that you wish you could tell your younger podcasting self?

Draft episodes in bulk! At the beginning of my podcast, I was brimming with creativity and had so many ideas for episodes. However, after about a year, I wasn't constantly coming up with new ideas each week; my creativity ebbed and flowed. Running a weekly show can get to be a lot and it's not realistic that you'll be churning out great episode ideas 100% of the time. So now, when I'm feeling particularly inspired and have several episode ideas, I write them out in full so I have episodes ready to go and don't panic if I'm feeling stuck one week. It makes podcasting so much easier!

Name: Jim Plotner

Time as a podcaster: A year

Show: Fan in the Van

'Stay safe mask up'

What do you wish you knew before starting podcasting?

How hard it is to gain followers and listeners but just gotta stay consistent and keep promoting.

♪

What's the biggest hack you've learned that you wish you could tell your younger podcasting self?

Not to worry about numbers just do it cause you love it and have fun with it.

Name: Breaking Down The Tape

Time as a podcaster: 2 years

Show: Breaking Down The Tape

'I said what I said'

What do you wish you knew before starting podcasting?

I wish I knew how to market my podcast organically. I started from scratch and learning to edit and record was easy enough, but learning how to grow organically was the main hurdle.

🎙

What's the biggest hack you've learned that you wish you could tell your younger podcasting self?

Joining podcasting communities. There is so much knowledge and amazing people out there that want to share it. The biggest hack is learning from others.

Name: CJ Ives Lopez

Time as a podcaster: Since 2019

Show: CJ

'Where Every Good Conversation Happens'

What do you wish you knew before starting podcasting?

I wish I knew how much work it was. Not that I would shy away from it, but I would have invested more into in the beginning instead of over time. I literally wanted to talk that was it so I started in 2019 talking with my sister on our SisterSisterLiveShow and it was great. Then I had the great idea of starting The Authors Porch. I absolutely love talking. I had CJ In The Morning. The audio was horrible in the beginning, the internet was spotty, but I didn't give up, I kept going and getting better. I took a Communication Acceleration course through Master Talk with Brenden Kumarasamy.

🎙

What's the biggest hack you've learned that you wish you could tell your younger podcasting self?

Be authentic and learn how to talk in front of the camera. If you watched some of the beginning video's of mine you would absolutely laugh. You can see my eyes go wide when my sister would say something and I would get embarrassed and think we had to be a specific way. I laugh sometimes and even apologize to my sister because I was trying to be something I was not. People are brutal and whether you are in front of a camera or just behind the microphone your true self can be heard no matter what. You can't fake it until you make it and you sure as hell will be felt through that microphone. Find what your niche is and what drives your passion and fuels your fire, then talk about it. That is how you make something great.

Name: Jenny Dang

Time as a podcaster: 11+ years

Show: Dante & Jenny Streaming

'Stop Scrolling and Start Streaming'

What do you wish you knew before starting podcasting?

We wish someone told us to stop over thinking and just start podcasting.

Before podcasting, we felt unsure about what we wanted the podcast to be about.

We knew we wanted to discuss popular streaming content such as documentaries/films/tv shows everyone had access to on platforms such as Netflix, Hulu, HBO Max, etc., but we wanted to do it in a way where we could be ourselves, have fun, connect, and provide value to our listeners.

After a few back and forth discussions, Dante and I decided to overcome our hesitations by hitting record and doing our best to hit every single one of those goals.

What we learned along the way was that by taking action and sharing our message meets insights, we were able to craft our show to be a journey where we can help our audience decide on what content they would want to watch as well as go deeper with our message to them by connecting that content with the world we live in.

We started with the idea that all our episodes needed to be perfect, but after reviewing our listener data, we actually realized the most popular ones were the ones that weren't perfect at all.

Technology and polished content has convinced many of us that we need to present ourselves to some sort or perfect standard, but in reality, the only important standard is to be true to yourself.

Once we started creating more podcast episodes with that in mind, podcasting no longer felt like "content creation," but a therapeutic way to connect with our audience authentically and have more conversations we aim to help others as well.

What's the biggest hack you've learned that you wish you could tell your younger podcasting self?

People come to me all the time super hung up on technology and use it as a reason to not start their podcast and/or share it.

If I could travel back in time and offer my younger podcasting self advice, I'd tell myself: "the equipment doesn't matter to get you going: just hit record and send.

Don't overthink it or stand in your own way, the world is always ready for your message.

Name: Harley Newell

Time as a podcaster: 8 months

Show: Murder Incorporated

'💯 % of listeners have not been murdered'

What do you wish you knew before starting podcasting?

I wish that I knew before I started podcasting what a challenging commitment that it would truly be. I would have banked more episodes before I started releasing them.

🎙

What's the biggest hack you've learned that you wish you could tell your younger podcasting self?

The biggest hack that I have learned is that the best way to grow your podcast audience (in my experience) is to befriend many other podcasters and go on as many podcasts as possible to get your name out there. Going on someone's podcast or show is free and it's the best advertisement that you will ever get for your show

Name: Stephen A. Schrum

Time as a podcaster: 3 years

Show: Audio Chimera

'A subversive podcast taking refuge in The Sanctuary of Allegory about the fragility of memory'

What do you wish you knew before starting podcasting?

The main thing to consider is how much time it takes. Of course, I resisted starting podcasting because I didn't think I had enough time; if you listen to my introductory episode I say exactly that! And now, four seasons later, I still need to figure out a better way to schedule creating new episodes.

What's the biggest hack you've learned that you wish you could tell your younger podcasting self?

For my podcast, it's really a do-it-myself project. And so I have developed kind of a workflow for writing, recording, and editing that works repeatedly episode after episode. (And again, if I just had more time for each of those phases!)

Name: Rajiv

Time as a podcaster: 1 year

Show: The Rajiv Show

'It's more than a show, welcome to my world.'

What do you wish you knew before starting podcasting?

Just start and figure it out along the way, perfection can come later.

Ǫ

What's the biggest hack you've learned that you wish you could tell your younger podcasting self?

Collab, collab, and more collaborations!

Name: Simona Costantini

Time as a podcaster: 3 years

Show: Happiness Happens Podcast

'Happiness Happens when you're least expecting it!'

What do you wish you knew before starting podcasting?

If I were to start my podcast all over again, I would focus more on understanding who my niche and target market is, and what the main things they would want to hear from me are. I started my show as a reflection of what I was going through and experiencing, in hopes that it would help just one other person; therefore, I wasn't as dialled into what my audience was resonating with as I am now.

With this in mind, I would also be clear on what my podcast goals are. Some people want to reach millions, some want to make hundreds of thousands of dollars, and some want to do it for fun and passion. It's so important to know what you want to get out of your podcasting experience and truly understand your 'why', because this is what will keep you grounded and guided as you continue on your podcast journey.

What's the biggest hack you've learned that you wish you could tell your younger podcasting self?

The biggest podcast hack I've learned is to find a system that works and stick with it. For me, I manage all of the podcast production in Trello, and I've hired out editing and social media content creation, which has resulted in more ears on my episodes. If you can't afford to hire both of these things out, pick what you really love to do, and see how much it would cost to hire out the things you don't love. When you stay doing the things you love to do, it never feels like work. So, outsourcing is important, and so is having a production system. It makes things so much easier, and now I'm 4 months ahead of schedule. Having my time freed up like this allows me to take the stress out of producing the podcast.

Name: Kayla Enslin

Time as a podcaster: 7 years

Show: Active FM

'Radio Has Never Been Better'

What do you wish you knew before starting podcasting?

Looking back now, I wish I knew it would take consistency and a whole lot of patience. It may not take off as quickly as you'd planned or hoped for. Keep growing in your skill, consistently bring out shows and keep looking for new ways to get your show out there.

What's the biggest hack you've learned that you wish you could tell your younger podcasting self?

Prepare thoroughly before you record the show and then relax and enjoy the recording!

Name: Nigel Beckles

Time as a podcaster: 18 months

Show: Interesting Conversations with Interesting People

'Featuring a wide variety of people with intriguing stories to share.'

What do you wish you knew before starting podcasting?

The importance of marketing.

🎙

What's the biggest hack you've learned that you wish you could tell your younger podcasting self?

Learning more about marketing podcasts.

Name: Delia Pena-Gay

Time as a podcaster: 10 months

Show: Just B You Podcast

'You are strong, you are worthy, you are enough'

What do you wish you knew before starting podcasting?

One thing I wish I'd learn is to look at my show as a laboratory. See yourself as a mad scientist: experiment with ideas, have fun, don't get attached to the ideas that didn't work. Most importantly KEEP GOING!! A show is like a person, it evolves and can have a life of its own. We live in a world that craves instant gratification, and applies pressure to keep up with trends. Just remember that your voice matters!

You are strong, you are worthy, you are enough.

🎙

What's the biggest hack you've learned that you wish you could tell your younger podcasting self?

Quality over quantity, and I'm not just talking about the sound!

Baby girl this is your show so make it what you want it to be. The numbers aren't what you want right now but remain true to the vision. Stand firm in every episode you make because that's what separates you from the rest.

Name: Howard Casner

Time as a podcaster: 1 1/2 years

Show: Pop Art

'Pop Art, where I find the pop culture in art and the art in pop culture.'

What do you wish you knew before starting podcasting?

The one thing I didn't really talk to people about is what host service to use. I simply went with one that a podcast used that I was often a guest on. But I had trouble with it in getting my podcast on Apple/iTunes, so I found another. But now I'm sort of stuck using both and would like to get rid of one of them. If I had more information beforehand, I would have gone with my second choice. The biggest challenge to me as a podcaster is that I have so little technical knowledge so it gets in the way of doing some things I'd like to do. There are some areas that I and other podcasters find frustrating: how to turn an mp3 file to mp4 for YouTube; how to find out how any followers you have on some streaming services like iTunes; etc.

What's the biggest hack you've learned that you wish you could tell your younger podcasting self?

My podcast is one with a guest for each episode. So while much of it is a discussion, there are moments when I just give out information. I have learned that I save a lot of time and effort if I have these bits written down in some form and more or less read them. They make these areas easier to edit since there are no "likes", "ands", "uhs", etc. to remove and I don't have to edit for focus and extraneous words and phrasing. Also, the more you edit, the more you recognize "uhs" so it becomes quicker to get rid of them in editing.

Name: Agi Keramidas

Time as a podcaster: Over 3 years

Show: Personal Development Mastery

'Stand out, don't fit in!

What do you wish you knew before starting podcasting?

For me podcasting started as a hobby, a joyous exploration. Later on it became a passion, and eventually my mission.

I took the route of exploring every aspect of podcasting myself, learning and doing everything myself. I enjoyed it and I learned a lot; however there was a significant time invested. I didn't know then how much time I would be devoting.

So this is probably one thing that I'd do differently (if any). See my next answer.

What's the biggest hack you've learned that you wish you could tell your younger podcasting self?

You don't need to do every aspect of the podcast yourself! See which elements you like doing, and keep doing them. The elements you do as a chore, delegate as soon as you can.

Name: Ryan Sullivan

Time as a podcaster: 3.5 years

Show: BopCast

'Interviewing Outliers and Those Breaking the Mold Regardless of the Status Quo'

What do you wish you knew before starting podcasting?

Consistency is the #1 thing you have to do. Stopping and starting will hurt you the most when it comes to podcasts and content. Every show I've worked on that failed, stopped before they got a chance to get off the ground - even when we had 5 celebrity guests. You have to stay consistent #1 for yourself, to hold yourself accountable #2 for your audience, because you're making a pact to them that in return for their time, you're giving them content that's useful #3 for any potential fan, guest, relationship that will happen in the future.

What's the biggest hack you've learned that you wish you could tell your younger podcasting self?

Delegate - hire people to do stuff you don't want to do.

Name: Alycia

Time as a podcaster: Since August 2020

Show: Civics & Coffee

History, in the time it takes to enjoy a cup of coffee.

What do you wish you knew before starting podcasting?

However long you think it will take you, double it. If you're wanting to build a community, you'll need to do more than put out consistent content. Just putting out content will take a lot of time. Depending on your niche, you'll need to research, map out your episode, record, edit and post it to your RSS feed. But you also need to get the word out which will require engaging in like-minded forums and social media platforms. And it will take work; you may not see immediate results in terms of downloads. But the longer you go at it, the more trust you'll build with your audience and the listens will come. I would also suggest thinking long and hard about why you're doing the podcast to begin with. If it's to make money, really consider another avenue. While there are opportunities to make some money, most are not self-sustaining on their show alone. I started mine as a hobby and it has been an absolute joy when I do get an occasional donation.

What's the biggest hack you've learned that you wish you could tell your younger podcasting self?

You can edit as you go through the first listen. When I started, I would listen once through, writing down the time stamps of where edits were needed, then go in and cut / edit those pieces one by one and then listen again. Now I listen once and cut as I go. Such a time saver!

Name: James Caton

Time as a podcaster: 6 months

Show: James & Co: The AI IOT Chronicles

What do you wish you knew before starting podcasting?

Don't sweat the numbers. whatever number of listeners you get, it's more than before you started podcasting. And, take that number (whatever it is) over the first 10 episodes, and think about how large a room you would need physically to fill it. maybe it's 50 people. maybe 200, or 350.

Think of that. you have filled a conference room full of people, willing to listen to your podcast.

That's pretty cool.

What's the biggest hack you've learned that you wish you could tell your younger podcasting self?

Just start.

Name: Anthony Jeannot

Time as a podcaster: 10 months

Show: Highbrow Drivel

'Hilarious conversations with serious experts'

What do you wish you knew before starting podcasting?

The cleaner and more professional your audio, the more likely people are to share your show. I was a big 'average audio can be overcome by great content' person, as my show slowly grew I started getting emails on my website about my audio from people saying they loved the show but didn't feel proud sharing it with a friend because the audio was a bit echoey and unprofessional. I still do all the editing myself and record remotely, but a £60 mic and a couple of hours on Youtube has greatly reduced the number of emails like that I get now.

🎙

What's the biggest hack you've learned that you wish you could tell your younger podcasting self?

Don't let being new limit the guests you ask to come on your show. I ask all kinds of scientists, politicians etc on the show. And only a very small percentage say yes, but if you ask 500 of the leaders in your field to be on your show and 10% of them say yes... Then you have a years worth of content from people in the top 500 in your field. Don't wait until your audience is huge, instead be smart, look at who has something to promote and have a clear value you can promote to them for how your show will help them reach a different audience to their usual crowd.

Name: JV Torres

Time as a podcaster: 5 years

Show: The Rise of King Asilas

'America under the rule of a king.'

What do you wish you knew before starting podcasting?

It's better to invest more time than money when starting out.

🎙

What's the biggest hack you've learned that you wish you could tell your younger podcasting self?

Use effects to change your voice so you can increase the amount of voices you can work with on your show.

Name: PH Murder Stories Podcast - Team

Time as a podcaster: 1 year

Show: PH Murder Stories

'Shocking, sad, revealing, and deeply researched, PH Murder Stories podcast covers the true account of infamous killings and true crime stories from the Philippines.'

What do you wish you knew before starting podcasting?

When we started launching our podcast, we really didn't know how to implement the social media aspect of promoting our content. We also did not know how to utilize podcast platforms and YouTube effectively. We had to research, watch tutorials, and seek help from fellow podcasters, who were already knowledgeable about how these things work. So our advice to new podcasters is to learn more about the utilization of social media in promoting a specific content (if you want to get as many listens as you can).

What's the biggest hack you've learned that you wish you could tell your younger podcasting self?

Based on our experience, we started very slow with reaching out to others, we could say that our anxiety got the best of us, because as a team, we were all not so sure about asking our family and friends to support us because we felt like our content was not as good as we expected. But along the way there were other podcasters that reached out to us and helped us with how to improve our content, the nuances to avoid, etc. So what we can say to new podcasters is that to reach out to people that are already in the podcasting industry, don't be shy also to ask your relatives and friends to heavily promote your podcast as it will grow for sure.

Name: Action Packed Travel

Time as a podcaster: 18 months

Show: Action Packed Travel

'Travel without having to go anywhere'

What do you wish you knew before starting podcasting?

How difficult it would be to find interesting guests.

What's the biggest hack you've learned that you wish you could tell your younger podcasting self?

Save your intro and outro separately.

Name: Denny Luce

Time as a podcaster: August 2014

Show: Tap the Craft Podcast

'Approachable craft beer educational podcast'

What do you wish you knew before starting podcasting?

When you first start a podcast you are enthusiastic and want to put out content for your listeners...so you push yourself to put out content on a weekly basis. The problem is the podcast begins to consume your free time. The important people around you are supportive in the beginning, but as the show goes on this begins to wear on their patience and they begin to resent the show. This was the case in the first podcast I hosted on a weekly basis for 3 years. When I started thinking about starting up a new podcast, I didn't want the burden of a weekly show...the burden on myself of having to come up with content, scheduling the recording and editing the episode and the burden on my family of sacrificing that time with them each week. So I compromised with putting out a new episode every other week. A bi-weekly schedule really helps keep you excited for each episode and doesn't wear on you as quickly. We are now a quarter way through our 8th year and we have never missed a bi-weekly release...and my marriage is still intact, so it is working out well.

What's the biggest hack you've learned that you wish you could tell your younger podcasting self?

Not sure it's a hack, but invest in a quality microphone as soon as you can. Make sure you understand how to set up the gain correctly so you are not too low and definitely not clipping. The content will bring new listeners, the quality of the content helps sustain those downloads, but if the audio quality is poor, even fantastic content won't keep them coming back.

Name: Ew

Time as a podcaster: 1year and 2 Months

Show: Chew & Ew Podcast

'Featuring RGV Talent and Texas Talent.'

What do you wish you knew before starting podcasting?

To prepare a back-up plan for formatting the podcast when the guest doesn't show.

🎤

What's the biggest hack you've learned that you wish you could tell your younger podcasting self?

Don't think about it, cause when you do you will run out of things to talk about. Focal points are the key to keep talking.

Name: Nick Atte

Time as a podcaster: 1 year 3 months

Show: Little Bits Of Stuff Podcast

'Getting you closer to your doctors'

What do you wish you knew before starting podcasting?

Podcasting is a work of passion, and consistency is key to unravelling your potential in every way possible. Don't limit yourself to a small box, the answer(s) a podcaster needs is usually better if it is spontaneous.

🎙

What's the biggest hack you've learned that you wish you could tell your younger podcasting self?

Just talk, it's natural to make mistakes. Let it flow and you'd do a better delivery.

Name: SJ Childs

Time as a podcaster: 7 months

Show: The SJ Childs Show

'Bringing value to families through education and resources'

What do you wish you knew before starting podcasting?

Just Do It that's how you get over the fear.

🎙

What's the biggest hack you've learned that you wish you could tell your younger podcasting self?

You're your own boss.

Name: Kira Dineen

Time as a podcaster: 11 years

Show: DNA Today

'Discover New Advances in the world of genetics.'

What do you wish you knew before starting podcasting?

Fake it until you make it! I started podcasting in high school and it was a lot of trial and error. Be kind with yourself as you make mistakes and learn from them. Bring the energy and enthusiasm to your show, the rest will follow.

There are endless resources now are a newbie podcaster. Take advantage of these webinars, clubhouse broadcasts, other podcasts, social media groups and more.

Don't be afraid to reach out to guests with a large following. The worst that will happen is that you don't get an answer. The best is that they come on your show and draw a new (and hopefully large) audience!

What's the biggest hack you've learned that you wish you could tell your younger podcasting self?

Record and produce episodes ahead of time. By staying ahead about 3 months this provides a cushion in case you experience roadblocks like struggling to book a guest, a guest cancels last minute, or life in general gets busy. This also gives you time to create and schedule social media posts, write the accompanying blog post, and provide information to your guest about the release of the episode.

Name: Thomas Nance

Time as a podcaster: 3 years

Show: OK Boomer

'With a comedic bent, Boomer and his spastic sidekick Jimmy Omadoufous, converse with people about their unusual professions.'

What do you wish you knew before starting podcasting?

Be patient. Numbers will grow slowly. Set a schedule and stick to it. I found publishing only twice a month allowed me to not burn out (so far).

🎤

What's the biggest hack you've learned that you wish you could tell your younger podcasting self?

I wish I had known earlier about the software called "The Levelator." It evens out volume of different levels between you, guest, and other inputs. It's free, it works, and it saves time!

Name: Trevor Lane

Time as a podcaster: 2-3 years

Show: Man Tools

'Remodel your Life!'

What do you wish you knew before starting podcasting?

Consistency is key. Whether you decide to release daily, weekly, or monthly... stick to that as much as humanly possible. If you're consistent the listens/views will come.

What's the biggest hack you've learned that you wish you could tell your younger podcasting self?

I haven't discovered any hacks. LOL. We've found that striving for consistent quality content is THE hack.

Name: Christopher Aggett

Time as a podcaster: 1 year and 8 months. (175 shows!)

Show: The Writing Community Chat Show

'The WCCS - TOGETHER AS ONE WE GET IT DONE.'

What do you wish you knew before starting podcasting?

Podcasting is really a journey. It is all about learning and developing as you go. As someone who jumped into the deep end, I do feel I have managed to do well. But there are things that I wish I knew before starting. For example, one method that could prove valuable is taking your time. What I mean by this is preparing your release ahead of time. This could be a number of things. Having an early marketing plan could help your show do well in regards to analytics and chart position on release. Most importantly, have a backlog of shows recorded and produced ready for launch day. It has been said that releasing 3 shows on launch day does wonders for its visibility. This is beneficial for many obvious reasons but by taking your time and being organised prior to your launch date, it gives you the opportunity to reflect time and time again. Every time you look something over you have the opportunity to improve it or enhance you strategy. So by taking that time and being patient could make the difference between a listener who switches off and one that sticks around.

What's the biggest hack you've learned that you wish you could tell your younger podcasting self?

I would most certainly tell myself to enjoy it and don't think about the numbers. Thats it really. When you start thinking about every stat it really diverts from the quality of show and you can only focus on the numbers. This is not productive and can really make the process stressful. I love my show and hosting it is so much fun, it is not worth worrying about the amount of listeners. I would say, if you are having fun, the audience will be having fun too.

Name: Russell Osborne

Time as a podcaster: 4 years

Show: Three Lions Podcast

'Independent England football supporters podcast'

What do you wish you knew before starting podcasting?

Possibly how much time and dedication it would take to consistently produce something that not only I'm happy with but also something that people will take the time to consume.

🎙

What's the biggest hack you've learned that you wish you could tell your younger podcasting self?

There is no need for high end expensive equipment, time, energy and soundproofing are all that's required.

Name: Joe from the Diz Hiz

Time as a podcaster: 2 years

Show: Diz Hiz

'The Disney History Podcast'

What do you wish you knew before starting podcasting?

I wish I knew more about audio and how audio worked. Not just levels, but how sound REALLY works. It is important to have good sound quality and through the past two years, myself and one of my co-hosts, have really learned a lot and are continuing to learn everyday how to make our sound quality better and are trying to become more efficient. Like good old Scrooge McDuck likes to say, Work Smarter, Not Harder!

What's the biggest hack you've learned that you wish you could tell your younger podcasting self?

Make connections with your listeners, because some of them will become life long friends and supporters!

Name: Bob Johnson

Time as a podcaster: 3 years

Show: Planet 8

'Podcast of the Fantastic!'

What do you wish you knew before starting podcasting?

We really had no idea about podcasting at the time. We were having monthly "Monster Club Lunches" where a group of us would get together and just talk about things we love. Monsters, science fiction, comics, etc.

One day I realized that there was a lot of knowledge around that table and it might be cool to share it beyond the walls of the restaurants.

No one wanted to commit to a monthly recording session, so the idea died for a bit. Until Larry Kakos mentioned wanting to do one. So, we got together with a mutual friend Karen Walker and started the Planet 8 Podcast.

I had the technical knowledge to record and edit the show. We spoke to a podcaster, Kyle Yount, who go us up and running on the Internet and on podcasting platforms.

I think if there was one thing I wish we knew more about at that time (and even now) it would be the marketing aspect of podcasting. When people hear our show, they tend to be very complimentary and really enjoy it. So, I know we have a good product. It is just a constant struggle to get the word out and get listeners to tune in and stream.

We push it online, but unlike many out there, we are older, so still do "analog tactics" like postcards, posters, listener parties and other physical forms of promotion. Local TV and radio, etc.

We love podcasting and enjoy what we do. It's just doing what we can to push it is where I would have loved to know more.

🎤

What's the biggest hack you've learned that you wish you could tell your younger podcasting self?

Not to spend endless hours editing out things like uhms and uhs and dead air. I still truncate the silent parts, but sometimes the "filler words" are a natural part of the conversation and it is better to mind them while recording than to remove them after.

This has cut down my editing time by at least a third. It also allows me more time on production aspects to make it a better overall experience. It doesn't have to be perfect, just entertaining.

Name: Frank Salvato

Time as a podcaster: 20 Years

Show: Underground USA

'No Fear. No Political Correctness.'

What do you wish you knew before starting podcasting?

In the beginning, before the term podcast was even coined and audio had to be hosted on your own website, acquiring traffic was about driving readers to your website. Since then, this process has branched out to include syndication platforms.

Having had to morph mindsets from webpage to exploiting social media, looking back, I would have liked to have understood much more about dissemination; getting "ears on audio," as it were.

While the processes are the same fundamentally with bringing a website up through the rankings, there is a lot more to getting a podcast heard increasingly by the masses. Having a solid grasp of the differences and the avenues required to advance ratings on a podcast would have been helpful.

What's the biggest hack you've learned that you wish you could tell your younger podcasting self?

Diligence and regularity. Find your voice (read: your niche) and stick to it with regularity. Don't waffle and think you can just pick it up again next week or tomorrow. If you are scheduled for a weekly then you have to show up and get it done.

Name: Rachel Lemley

Time as a podcaster: Six months

Show: Inzomniac

'True crime, history, ghost stories and folklore all in one place!'

What do you wish you knew before starting podcasting?

I wish that I had known how to better market.

🎙

What's the biggest hack you've learned that you wish you could tell your younger podcasting self?

Just keep going, stay regular with releases and keep creating.

Name: Chaniera Stewart

Time as a podcaster: 4 years

Show: Uncommon Women Podcast

'Stay Uncommon'

What do you wish you knew before starting podcasting?

You can't just record and post on streaming apps, great content brings more listeners.

🎙

What's the biggest hack you've learned that you wish you could tell your younger podcasting self?

Take your time and the viewers will come don't get impatient and family and friends aren't your only support step out and find new supporters who believe in what you're doing.

Name: Nolan G

Time as a podcaster: 1 year

Show: Every Podcast I Love is dead

'Rock.metal.punk'

What do you wish you knew before starting podcasting?

Overnight success doesn't just happen. If you expect to drop a podcast and have 1000 downloads or even 100 immediately you will be disappointed right out of the gate. Take the time to build it, get better with each episode, try new things build out your social media and connect with fellow podcasters. Ultimately you may never get to 1000 downloads but you will enjoy the journey a whole lot more.

🎙

What's the biggest hack you've learned that you wish you could tell your younger podcasting self?

Don't be afraid to reach out to that guest for an onterview. The worst they can say is no, or not respond but more often than not they will say yes, or at least provide you with a guest who is willing to come on your show.

Name: Kevin

Time as a podcaster: 6-7 yrs

Show: Left at the Valley, left at the Valley 2.0

'You are not alone'

What do you wish you knew before starting podcasting?

It's okay to lose control of the creative side, sometimes giving co-host a free license to make a segment their own bring unexpected surprises, always have a back up guest or show because people will cancel last minute on you, have a minimum knowledge of the tech and you can't have a contingency for everything.

What's the biggest hack you've learned that you wish you could tell your younger podcasting self?

Talking with people is easier and less scary than talking to people.

Name: Shark Files

Time as a podcaster: 5 months

Show: Shark Files

'Telling the true stories of when shark and human lives collide'

What do you wish you knew before starting podcasting?

I wish I'd known how much time and effort promotion of the podcast would take. Early on you need to really fight for every listen and it's been hard at times to balance those demands with focusing properly on the actual product itself. As I have a scripted narrative podcasted it takes a lot of research and writing to produce, so if I'd been aware I would have stockpiled more episodes before launching to give myself more time for promotion and marketing.

🎤

What's the biggest hack you've learned that you wish you could tell your younger podcasting self?

Get involved in communities relating to your podcast's topic on Facebook, Reddit and other social media sites and build a network. Become a regular presence and an authority on your subject within those communities, whether it's true crime or fashion. Interacting as '_____ podcast', you'll draw potential listeners- free advertising basically- to your show by answering peoples' questions, posting interesting content, and joining in on discussions.

Name: The Dhiya Talks

Time as a podcaster: 1 year

Show: The Dhiya Talks

'Relatable stuffs comedy podcast | Top stand up comedy podcast from itunes'

What do you wish you knew before starting podcasting?

Being a podcaster for the past one year made me realise many truths, and a lot more to unlock. The first thing is, NEVER ever start a podcast for the sake of earning an immediate income, you need passion and patience for it. The next is the production part, it's tougher than I thought, unless and until you know something about recording, editing and marketing. And obviously the last one is marketing part, I didn't knew you need the same effort of recording to market a podcast as well. Distribute it like crazy (thank me later).

🎙

What's the biggest hack you've learned that you wish you could tell your younger podcasting self?

Stick onto a particular niche, have a good content and be CONSISTENT. Never give up because you don't know what awaits you ;)

Name: Mike Bivens

Time as a podcaster: 2 years

Show: Smart Contracts Decoded

'Understanding Smart Contracts and their use cases.'

What do you wish you knew before starting podcasting?

The main thing I wish I knew before I started podcasting was the significance of community. Not necessarily creating one around your brand or your podcast, but engaging and participating in others that are built around and focused on your topic(s). Utilizing these spaces to grow your network and knowledge base, find guests, and to connect with others meaningfully ensures that you can drive organic growth to your show while contributing to the topic at a different level.

This level of participation signals to others that you care and are a source of entertainment or knowledge that would otherwise be locked to you. I highly encourage any podcaster to identify relevant communities and learn how they can engage in those spaces to contribute and expand your presence and impact on the topic.

What's the biggest hack you've learned that you wish you could tell your younger podcasting self?

The biggest hack I learned that I wish I knew when I started podcasting is the ability to accept starting a new podcast and leaving behind the old one. I'm now on my fourth podcast and I've held a lot of guilt getting to this point after putting in so much work on each show and trying to walk away. I struggled with the feeling of abandoning projects I believed in and with feeling like it's been a series of failures. But, after looking back it's because I went through so much effort that this new show will be the best yet and I can take the collective lessons from each to minimize issues and maximize processes and value.

Name: Kawan Karadaghi

Time as a podcaster: 6 months

Show: ValueVerse Podcast (name changing in a few weeks)

'Stories of work/life.'

What do you wish you knew before starting podcasting?

Not trying to be like someone else and the show they're doing. Trying to be someone else because you enjoyed their podcast and want to be like them isn't doing you justice. Being yourself and talking about what you like can be heard and is an enjoyable podcast to listen to when the host is playing to his strengths. Also outsourcing editing to a editor on Upwork or Fiverr a lot sooner, this freeing up of time can prevent "podfade" and allowing you to focus on what you love to do, which is talking to great guests. Outsource a few episodes if you can, if not the whole thing. So you can focus on the good stuff and not get bogged down with tech and chores that can make podcasting not fun.

What's the biggest hack you've learned that you wish you could tell your younger podcasting self?

Using TidyCal as a calendar scheduler for guests, its the cheapest and confirms your guests via email automatically for you at no extra cost. Guest research. Know your guest, don't try to just wing the podcast. Take the minimum of thirty minutes to an hour and study your guest. This insight will allow you to ask better questions and provide a much better show. I've also learned that shows under thirty minutes get more downloads.

Name: Max Chan

Time as a podcaster: January 2021

Show: Chan With A Plan

'Providing career advice in easy actionable steps, for frustrated professionals, helping you overcome career challenges so you can stop feeling confused and defeated and start feeling focused and confident in order to excel in your career.'

What do you wish you knew before starting podcasting?

Creating a consistent podcast isn't only one factor to consider. If you want a loyal podcast following, you need to build a community around it.

What's the biggest hack you've learned that you wish you could tell your younger podcasting self?

Optimize podcast titles, really helps increase your visibility and downloads for episodes.

Name: PNW Haunts & Homicides

Time as a podcaster: just under a year

Show: PNW Haunts & Homicides

'Have a creepy ass day!'

What do you wish you knew before starting podcasting?

Just how much work it is. Research how to set up your hosting platform - which one should you choose, what microphones and other equipment or services do you need? More research for your episodes, recording, editing, and that's only after you put in the work to be approved by the streaming platforms. Create an email account, or two. Establish a business entity if that's part of your established goals. Set up a business banking account. Manage the socials, promo swaps, collaborations on episodes, affiliate links and sponsorships. Patreon (or buymeacoffee)! Still haven't gotten to merch. It's all a little overwhelming but we love doing it. It's worth it when you love it and eventually see positive results.

What's the biggest hack you've learned that you wish you could tell your younger podcasting self?

Don't be too hard on yourself because nothing you create will be perfect but if it's uniquely you sometimes people surprise you with their response. There will always be one guy heckling from the back. Mostly people respond in overwhelmingly positive ways when it's truly a passion project for you because that just comes through.

Name: Barely

Time as a podcaster: 15 years

Show: Barely Podcasting

'Life isn't a spectator sport, this is the play-by-play'

What do you wish you knew before starting podcasting?

Find your passion and go! Don't worry too much about the best equipment, listenership, how everyone is doing it. Just hit record. Your show will evolve over time, but if you are worried about it being perfect from the first episode, you will fail.

The mistakes help you grow, and if you embrace them, it can actually help grow your audience, if you can find a way to incorporate them in to your show eventually. You will make mistakes, and lots of them. Don't get discouraged. Just hit record.

Make sure you are comfortable with your equipment, even if it is cheap to start off with. Equipment can be upgraded at a later date. Intros can be changed or totally re-imaged at a later date. Logos and imagery can be created and/or revamped days, months, or even years later. Unless you get really bad audio distortion, the audience will keep coming back as long as content is king. Just hit record.

There could be other shoes out there with the same basis, focus, or concentration. What they don't have is you and your interpretation of anything. Your style is unique. Be original, but true to yourself and the soul of your show. Just hit record.

Finally, don't overthink it. We can be paralyzed by fear and self doubt. This is new to you, it can be scary, but don't paralyze your efforts by getting stuck before you even try. Talk to other podcasters, both in and out of your niche. Most will gladly help someone starting up. Just hit record.

What's the biggest hack you've learned that you wish you could tell your younger podcasting self?

There are always new ways to try something. May times a free solution is right around the corner.

Name: Jennifer James and Jill Stanley

Time as a podcaster: 2 years

Show: Common Mystics

'Making the Extraordinary Ordinary'

What do you wish you knew before starting podcasting?

Be clear about why you want to be a podcaster, about what you want to accomplish by doing this work. Your purpose should be directly related to how you measure your success in the months and years to come.

When we started, we knew we wanted to share our adventures as road trip psychic sisters in search of untold (or "undertold") stories from the dead. Though we knew we wanted to share our stories, we didn't identify exactly what we wanted to accomplish by putting them out into the world. Was making money our ultimate goal? Did we want to drum up business for ourselves as psychic readers? Did we want to sell products and merchandise associated with the show? Or was the goal more spiritual in nature? Did we wish to share our stories as accessible examples of mystical work? Did we want to practice and strengthen our own psychic abilities? Did we simply want to give voice to the dead who spoke to us? Finally, was the goal to collaborate on a project as sisters? A project that would allow us to form a closer bond and validate each other's otherworldly experiences? We jumped into podcasting without asking these questions of ourselves or each other. Fast forward two years when the pandemic no longer allows us the luxury to work exclusively from home. When it's harder to find the time to travel, research, record and edit. When our listener numbers are waning. When we ask ourselves that inevitable question: Why are we doing this??? Had we answered that question before we started podcasting, it would have come easier now.

But, we regrouped and came up with our answer. We do this because we love to travel together and to practice our psychic abilities with each other. Our main goal is to have fun. So now we remind ourselves, and each other, of this goal, especially in light of listener data and other indicators that cannot measure it. Are we still having fun? If so, we are achieving our goal. We are a success.

What's the biggest hack you've learned that you wish you could tell your younger podcasting self?

We've stumbled upon some helpful tips when editing in Audacity. For example, it's much easier to edit a conversation when each speaker is recorded on a separate track. Also, recording remotely can be done with ease using a teleconference app; simply have each person record his/her own voice at their end and add them together on different tracks during production. You can use the Amplify effect to silence areas of sound that you want to remove, as this offers more flexibility than simply deleting.

Name: Trish the Dish

Time as a podcaster: Since August 2020

Show: GenX Voice

'Bridging generations using a forgotten generation as a bridge builder'

What do you wish you knew before starting podcasting?

I wish I knew so many things, but I have to say the biggest thing is that I wish I knew how amazing and inclusive the podcast community is! I would have started years before, when I first thought about it, instead of waiting so long. I could have gathered so much more support, tips, and tricks instead of stumbling through the first year. Although I did do a lot of research on my own, I wasted a lot of time, energy and especially money on poor decisions. Everything you want to know, and everyone you need to build a support system with is out there. Don't wait-look now! It is the best thing I found in podcasting. Even though you are sitting alone in a room with a microphone, there is a huge community out there wanting to see you thrive!

What's the biggest hack you've learned that you wish you could tell your younger podcasting self?

The right editing software saved me hours and hours of time! Get into those podcast communities and ask ask ask before you struggle with some janky software that comes on your computer. A lot of it is FREE!!!

Name: Holly Curby

Time as a podcaster: 1 year

Show: Holly's Highlights

'Encourage, inspire and equip listeners to intentionally live their life full of purpose'

What do you wish you knew before starting podcasting?

After a year of podcasting, the main thing I wish I knew before starting my podcast, Holly's Highlights, would be more about sound quality. Specifically about sound equipment for interviewing other people remotely so that it sounds clear and as if you are both in the same room. It truly can be hit or miss with interviews and which ones sound clear and which ones are soft and distanced - as if in a cave or a can. Sound quality is so crucial in the quality of a podcast and the listenership of that episode.

What's the biggest hack you've learned that you wish you could tell your younger podcasting self?

Plan - then when you plan, plan more! This way you have a schedule layed out of topics as well as backups for when that sponsor slows down the timeliness of getting out a podcast, or an interview is delayed due to health, or even an opportunity arises that you need to move them around. So glad I started with 5 episodes in the chute and try to stay ahead by a good 4 as I continue to record.

Name: Toby Brendel

Time as a podcaster: 10 years

Show: Tangents with Toby

What do you wish you knew before starting podcasting?

Wait for 5 years. Not much information about podcasting was out when I started!

What's the biggest hack you've learned that you wish you could tell your younger podcasting self?

Promote! Promote! Promote!

Name: Dave Barr

Time as a podcaster: Since August 2020

Show: The Real Life Buyer

'Save money and buy smart'

What do you wish you knew before starting podcasting?

Podcasting has been somewhat of a revelation for me as so many things have happened. To pick one is challenging though, when I think deeply about this, I feel I need to reflect inwards.

My career as a Purchasing professional has brought me into contact with many people but most have been with a focus on the commercial aspects of trade and negotiation, podcasting has enabled me to connect with individuals at a far more personal and deeper level. Many of my guests I would have never met in normal circumstances and the conversations we have held have covered subjects beyond business, operations and supply to include self development and self care. These discussions have inspired me to look at how I interact with people at a different level, grow as an individual, view others and contribute to the world.

I now spend less time watching TV, read way more, exercise every day, seek inspirational people and content, improve my media and creative skills, meditate, give and express gratitude but also consider others, the environment, society and the world in a more caring and purposeful way.

I love podcasting, what it has taught me and whom it has brought me.

🎙

What's the biggest hack you've learned that you wish you could tell your younger podcasting self?

Broaden your social media and creative skills and get comfortable with video as well as audio. Don't expect a static post here or there to be enough. Mix it up. Make videos. Get creative and be consistent.

Name: Miranda & Victoria

Time as a podcaster: Since November 2020

Show: The Animal Files

'Exposing the Truth, Science, & Spirituality of Pet Care'

What do you wish you knew before starting podcasting?

We wish that we had known that older computers (especially more than 3 years old) could cause issues with editing. A lot of lost time and headache could have been prevented with a newer computer. If possible.. upgrade your computer. Older computers can make the editing process slower and more glitchy.

🎙

What's the biggest hack you've learned that you wish you could tell your younger podcasting self?

Remember to save your work as you go. Make saving your work an obsessive habit. The most painful thing in editing is working for awhile and unexpectedly losing it all and having to start over due to a computer/software crash or a power outage.

Or...

Edit for your audience not for yourself. Listeners like real conversation. Don't be a perfectionist and over produce yourself. Keep in some of the natural conversational pauses and filler words. It's a much more pleasing listener experience. Your listener will feel like they are listening to a real conversation and will connect with you and your content a heck of a lot better.

Name: Arys Déjan

Time as a podcaster: 2 years!

Show: The Who & How Club

'Without you, without me, there is no we.'

What do you wish you knew before starting podcasting?

I wish I knew that I wouldn't need anyone else to co-host or build the brand that I have created now. My show went through 2 iterations before it became what it is today, and those first 2 versions of my show included people that didn't have the same vision as I did. Their hearts weren't in it. I thought I needed a host (went through 2) and they didn't work out. I thought I needed a production team, but they ended up just being in it for the money, so I had to restart twice...but you know what they say....3rd times a charm. And it really was and has been. I am currently at the safest place with my show, it feels safe. It's growing organically, it has formed into its theme and what I have always wanted it to represent. It has had many accolades in such a short period of time, and we have no one but the Podcast Gods and supporters to thank for this!

What's the biggest hack you've learned that you wish you could tell your younger podcasting self?

Making guest appearances on people's shows early on would've been something that I would tell my younger podcasting self. Ensuring that my face is everywhere, popping up on other people's platforms, in order to not only promote my own and my brand, but just me as a host, as a personality and an individual. This is paying off now, but if I started early with this 2 years ago, I may be at a different level and notoriety today. No regrets, though!

THE MELTING POT

Name: Sly & Kartier

Time as a podcaster: 2 years

Show: The Melting Pot

'If you can't Stand the Heat, Get out of the Kitchen'

What do you wish you knew before starting podcasting?

No one is going to care about your podcast just because it's there. I hear so often that people have no theme or agenda, they're just shooting around topics, and nobody is going to care about that unless you're already famous. If you want a podcast worth caring about, use your expertise, put in the research, and come up with ideas no one else has. We are far from being experts ourselves so we are not sure if this is applicable to everyone, but it's something a lot of podcasters need to hear before getting started. Building your brand and establishing your podcasts niche is essential when trying to stand out between thousands of podcasts.

What's the biggest hack you've learned that you wish you could tell your younger podcasting self?

Patience is the most important key to podcasting - It takes time for people to "get to know you." Your early episodes won't be great because you're going to want to sound like someone else and model other shows. Once you find your own voice, your own flow, and your own style... That's when you'll start to see traction. Also, with time comes more episodes, meaning that new people that discover you have more episodes to download. In the beginning, 1 new subscriber might equal 3 or 4 downloads.As time progresses so will your numbers. Time and patience are the BIGGEST key. Lastly, a new concept that we've been testing out has helped further us. We created a SubReddit at the Melting Pot where we post every new episode to our own SubReddit. We then encourage people to subscribe to the SubReddit on the podcast page.

RETAIL LEADERSHIP WITH STEVE WORTHY

Name: Steve Worthy

Time as a podcaster: 1 year

Show: Retail Leadership with Steve Worthy

'Retail Leaders impact everyone, every day all over the world'

What do you wish you knew before starting podcasting?

So two things: 1) I wish I had taken the time to hype up the launch of podcast. I should have dedicated about 4-6 weeks building up to its launch. I think I did 10 days.

2) Storytelling - learn this craft as a podcaster, it helps set you apart from other podcasters.

What's the biggest hack you've learned that you wish you could tell your younger podcasting self?

Create outlines for multiple episodes and batch record. Currently, I record 2-3 episodes at a time.

Name: Jessica Kumar

Time as a podcaster: 3 years

Show: Invisible India Podcast

'Navigating India With Love'

What do you wish you knew before starting podcasting?

Invest in audio quality right away.

What's the biggest hack you've learned that you wish you could tell your younger podcasting self?

Go ahead and record multiple episodes at a time and record episodes way in advance to release later. Not everything has to be real time.

BLAXIT GLOBAL

Name: Chrishan Wright

Time as a podcaster: 15 months

Show: Blaxit Global

'You've heard the term, now be inspired by the movement.'

What do you wish you knew before starting podcasting?

I wish I fully understood how long editing can take. At the end of my first season I hired an editor. Best decision.

What's the biggest hack you've learned that you wish you could tell your younger podcasting self?

I wish I could tell my younger podcasting self to push past the fear and do it anyway. You never know the impact your message will have if you don't record and publish.

STRONGWRITERS ON SONGWRITING

Name: EB Martin

Time as a podcaster: 3 months

Show: Strongwriters On Songwriting

'Inside the Song'

What do you wish you knew before starting podcasting?

I was certain my voice alone would ruin the whole thing, as a writer I believe I know how to tell a story, but as a host I had no experience whatsoever and felt very uncertain. I didn't like what I heard back after recording (my own voice). Soon enough I realized the success of the show had more to do with listening to my guests and responding in kind - the sound of my voice has less to do with producing a good podcast than I had imagined, I got over it quickly and actually feel very comfortable recording myself, with the realization: just say what you have to and allow your guest the space to shine, it is about them after all.

What's the biggest hack you've learned that you wish you could tell your younger podcasting self?

Simple, keep it simple. Find a format that works for you and stick to it.

TRUE BELIEVERS: A COMIC BOOK PODCAST

Name: True Believers: A Comic Book Podcast

Time as a podcaster: 2 months

Show: True Believers: A Comic Book Podcast

What do you wish you knew before starting podcasting?

I wish I knew how to have a proper set up. The best trick to sound quality is to find a quiet space to record where the sound won't bounce off the walls.

What's the biggest hack you've learned that you wish you could tell your younger podcasting self?

Social media is important to growing your listeners!

Name: Jeremy Grater

Time as a podcaster: 17 years

Show: The Fit Mess

'Learn from two vulnerable guys sharing fears and failures as the strive for better wellness.'

What do you wish you knew before starting podcasting?

Podcasting is an act of community building, not broadcasting your ideas to anyone lucky enough to find them. The more you give, the more you get.

What's the biggest hack you've learned that you wish you could tell your younger podcasting self?

Authentically engage in communities and social circles where people can benefit from what you're sharing. Online or in real life, give what you can and people will be drawn to your message.

THE BOOKSHELF ODYSSEY PODCAST

Name: Art Kilmer

Time as a podcaster: Year and a half

Show: The Bookshelf Odyssey Podcast

'It is a truth universally acknowledged, that a reader in possession of a good book, must be in want of another...'

What do you wish you knew before starting podcasting?

I wish I had known how easy it was to record a podcast - that I didn't need all the fancy expensive equipment to start with. I had wanted to start a podcast sooner than I did but I kept using my lack of "good" equipment and skill as an excuse. I have since learned that you can start simply: using your phone or laptop and with even an inexpensive microphone you can get a pretty good sound from it if you use good microphone technique. Use the equipment you have available to you, and then build on it and improve it as you get more experienced at podcasting.

What's the biggest hack you've learned that you wish you could tell your younger podcasting self?

I'm not sure this is a hack as much as it is advice: Don't be afraid to go to places like YouTube to help you find an answer to your question about equipment, technique, etc. But there can be so much information there it can be overwhelming - so I would say even more importantly: Don't be afraid to reach out to other podcasters asking for advice, equipment suggestions, etc. I felt like I had a huge learning curve when I started and was overwhelmed by all that I had to learn. I felt like I was just running in circles. Finally I built up the courage to reach out to a couple of podcasters who I greatly enjoyed asking for their help. They were so gracious and basically sent me a list of videos to watch on youtube that helped them figure out how to do all the technical things, efficiently and in a reasonably affordable way. They were able to narrow down the information for me and were able to give tried and true ways of doing things more effectively. I have since found that many podcasters love helping other podcasters. So to summarize: the biggest hack I've learned is to ask for help!

Name: The Slot Podcast

Time as a podcaster: 3 years

Show: The Slot Podcast

'Wentworth'

What do you wish you knew before starting podcasting?

Sponsors.

What's the biggest hack you've learned that you wish you could tell your younger podcasting self?

Podcasting editing isn't hard as you think.

HALSHACK INDIE ROCKCAST

Name: Hal Jester

Time as a podcaster: 7 years

Show: Halshack Indie Rockcast

'Best in rock, pop, and alternative anywhere!'

What do you wish you knew before starting podcasting?

Looking back on my crazy career there are many things I could have done differently but then would I have had the same results. I'm a bit of an anomaly in the music industry. I've had many clandestine moments of fate and coincidences that wouldn't have happened had I not been in the right place at the right time at the right moment. Almost like a path was being carved for me from the outside of the industry to the top.

I started this journey well over 7 years ago into the music biz but it was in 2014 I was offered my own show on a network in England after a few guest spots on a buddies show (Rango Unmuzzled aka Matthew Meadows) who was hosted on that network! I'm forever grateful for my launch on their network (REPUTATION RADIO)! I couldn't have done it without a support group to get me going.

Find yourself a group of like minded podcasters to get started with like I did but I was lucky! I wish I had known more about podcasting hosts but in 2014 there weren't many good ones or many at all for that matter because I started out on Fandalism hosted by You Tube. It was really hard to get going. I had many life problems and it took me 3 years to make my first 10 episodes but evidently that was supposed to happen because I landed a band out of California that asked to be on my show (Magic Giant) well a year later that band was popped by ROLLING STONE mag and I was already on them a year earlier!!!

(instant cred for me) so that in turn on landed me Frankie Muniz as a drummer in a band (KINGSFOIL) then on a fluke that landed me STEVIE NICKS exclusive song project "STAND BACK" from the PAPER JACKETS endorsed, approved and produced by Miss Nicks herself!!!! So these events have nothing to do with how I started and everything to do with how I started at the same time.

After I featured Magic Giant I found a podcast host to get started on PODOMATIC (they kept offering me deals to expand my space and bandwidth, there were so helpful early on) Now I'm on an expensive unlimited package with the company on a deal! (I will never leave). Get a good microphone, I started with a cheap headset mic...ughh!! Use CANVA to make your ads! Wish I knew about all those at the time! ABSOLUTELY make top grade content regardless of what it is! You don't want to be considered second best at anything! Be the best or don't do at all was my motto from the get go so my reputation was built strong early! Learn about #hashtagging on twitter and IG and FB! I learned that one early too. # on anything relevant to your show or topic. Find yourself some important people to back your show that will grow into more where you can get testimonials and post those on flyers and your website also social media of course.

Start on Buzzsprout or Podomatic! Get yourself a website on Weebly (which I did immediately in 2014) now I see 10,000 hits a month to my website! 15 pages and growing but its taken 7 years for a bunch of weird events to play out that have allowed me to progress! It's all talked about in my episodes and on the bios for each episode as well.

7 years later I'm heard in 350 markets around the world in 103 countries! Ive earned multiple accolades and endorsements from top stars like Duran Duran and Stevie Nicks plus NBC has come calling for some of my artists for a new TV show coming summer 2022 for original artists based on the wildly popular EUROVISION! Im super honored to have earned their support!

Hope this helps! Check out my show! The best hour of music anywhere anytime you listen with the occasional hosted episode my ME yours truly HALSHACK!

Every episode is as good or better than the last! That's the Halshack promise and guarantee!

"Change the music, change your attitude, change your life"....Halshack quote

🎙

What's the biggest hack you've learned that you wish you could tell your younger podcasting self?

Don't worry about getting tongue tied or tripped up or losing your train of thought. Not everything has to be cut in one take. You can hit the stop button and start again from where you screwed up. It can always be edited....lol. This is easier said than done when it's not a solo podcast. If you have cohosts or guests then this can be way more complicated but I would say something I started early (like very first show). I downloaded WAVEPAD to make my shows and edit. I wouldn't use anything else for a fledgling podcaster. I've used it for 7 years. I've tried others and I'm very pleased that I discovered that program at the onset.

JESS GET HIRED

Name: Jessica Fiesta George

Time as a podcaster: 1 year

Show: Jess Get Hired

'A podcast for jobseekers, business professionals, the underemployed and the unappreciated employee.'

What do you wish you knew before starting podcasting?

When decided to start podcasting, I thought I would record a few episodes and be done with it because nobody would listen. I'm into my 1st year and I'm in awe of the podcast community and my new found fans! Everyone has been so helpful. Main thing I wish I knew before podcasting is to do more research: about podcasting, about your niche, about your competition, about marketing, about content, and about how to hustle. You get what you put into it that's for sure. Going in with a clear mission and vision and plan is key!

What's the biggest hack you've learned that you wish you could tell your younger podcasting self?

I think I'm still learning so you tell me. LOL I would say however, networking and trying to be a guest or get a guest with a following is one of the keys to growth.

THE AUTHENTIC MILLENNIAL

Name: Dj Ace333

Time as a podcaster: 2 years

Show: The Authentic Millennial

'Motivating millennials to live a life of authenticity'

What do you wish you knew before starting podcasting?

Podcasting is a slow grind. The longer you do it, the better you get at podcasting without even realizing it.

What's the biggest hack you've learned that you wish you could tell your younger podcasting self?

Networking and relationships building are the two biggest things you can do for a podcast even if you don't release a podcast episode consistently.

CYPHER

Name: Michael

Time as a podcaster: 1 year

Show: Cypher

'The new voices in Hip-Hop.'

What do you wish you knew before starting podcasting?

Just have fun at first, I spent too much time trying to make a business before it ever was one.

What's the biggest hack you've learned that you wish you could tell your younger podcasting self?

People will feed off of your energy. You are the value-add to your own show and you are what makes it unique. You don't have to reinvent the wheel to have a good show.

THE #ASKTONY SHOW

Name: Tony Acosta

Time as a podcaster: Since 2014

Show: The #AskTony Show

What do you wish you knew before starting podcasting?

If I could somehow go back and talk to myself seven years ago the first thing I would say would be to find other podcasters and join their community. Podcasting was very lonely for me at first. I had few downloads, few interests, and what seemed like few reasons to continue at times. Attaching myself to a community of podcasters would have helped me grow and learn much quicker! That is the reason I, along with our team, started the Utah Podcast Coalition to create the very resource I wish I would have had access to when I started. Like anything in life, if you can find people who have more success and experience than you, that dramatically shortens the learning curve. At the end of the day, you don't know what you don't know and being in a room of podcasters has helped me make valuable tweaks and adjustments.

What's the biggest hack you've learned that you wish you could tell your younger podcasting self?

The number one hack that has helped me improve the quality of my show has been an organized show prep process. By taking the time to have a prep call with my guests I have improved the quality of the conversations and allowed the guests to have more input on the content which has made them feel more comfortable during our show. A lot of people get very nervous in front of a microphone and having and idea of the content of the interview has helped them be more calm and positive! It does take time and organization to do but it has been THE hack that has boosted the quality of my show. Not only does it prep the guest in terms of the content that will be presented but it also helps solidify and differentiate your show as a professional show with procedures and organization, guests value that tremendously.

DICKHEADS OF HISTORY

Name: Cian Tookey

Time as a podcaster: 1 1/2 years

Show: Dickheads of History

'Taking glamorised individuals in history and showing another side to them.'

What do you wish you knew before starting podcasting?

How important advertising is.

What's the biggest hack you've learned that you wish you could tell your younger podcasting self?

Starting promotion earlier.

THE LIGHT INSIDE

Name: Jeffrey Besecker

Time as a podcaster: Three years

Show: The Light Inside

'We're all on the journey to discover the light inside, that beacon which guides us to live our truest, most authentic self.'

What do you wish you knew before starting podcasting?

As I ponder the relatively quick rise of our podcast program, I am going to share what I feel to be the most valuable lesson for any podcast to embrace.

No podcasting skill can be more effective key utilized than understanding how to structure your show outlines to establish maximum impact with the message each episode shares with your listening community. Too frequently, podcasters feel they are at their best when they are unhinged from the guides of a script or outline.

Ability does offer one freedom to roll with the direction a guest might offer, yet it also leaves one at the mercy of straying u to long-winded ramble.

An effective host establishes the time and pace of subject exploration. A main topical direction and theme should be established throughout every step of the message creation process. Always establish the main point of any discussion and guide your conversation so the guest efficiently and effectively conveys this point.

What's the biggest hack you've learned that you wish you could tell your younger podcasting self?

(NOT SO) SECRET DADS BUSINESS

Name: Nate Robinson

Time as a podcaster: 13 months

Show: (not so) Secret Dads Business

'Taking the Secret Out of Fatherhood'

What do you wish you knew before starting podcasting?

As an independent podcaster, trying to fly by the seat of your pants with no real plan isn't the way to go. Focus on the stuff your audience doesn't see.

Set up a website, get a few episodes recorded in the bank before release and promote the podcast on social media or even guest spots on other shows to get people interested before you launch.

What's the biggest hack you've learned that you wish you could tell your younger podcasting self?

Set up a "template" of your show format for your editing. Take a note of times for your intro, sponsor ads and your episode itself. It will make it easier to put together for publishing.

Also, keep an eye on your analytics. Forget about your overall download numbers and focus on your audience retention for each episode.

Do you find your audience retention starts to regularly drop off after the 25 minute mark? Consider condensing your episodes down and making them shorter.

We live in a world of instant gratification and people get bored quickly. A short and engaging episode is sometimes better than a drawn out informative episode.

CONTENT MARKETING HACKS

Name: Asyraaf Fero

Time as a podcaster: 2 years

Show: Content Marketing Hacks

'Content creator gets likes, but content marketer gets paid'

What do you wish you knew before starting podcasting?

Know how to monetize the podcast as early as possible. I didn't know there's a way to do that until I learn it from someone who monetize the podcast even before launching it. Now that I know this method, I felt like I left tons of money on the table before.

What's the biggest hack you've learned that you wish you could tell your younger podcasting self?

Know your ideal client, not ideal listener, because when you're thinking about client, you'd change the monetization approach and you could make money early without waiting for 12 months building audience and publish consistently. If you have a business, then making money fast should be your priority. Another thing is, treat every episode like a sales letter. It's the purpose to sell your offer. And that's how you turn a podcast into a money machine that works for you 24/7.

BEYOND RETIREMENT

Name: Jacquie Doucette

Time as a podcaster: Since May 2019

Show: Beyond Retirement

'It's Your Life ... Live It!'

What do you wish you knew before starting podcasting?

When I first started podcasting, I thought it was going to be important to plan out all my episodes ahead of time. I spent hours pondering what I was going to talk about and how to say it so it made the most sense. I didn't realize that the majority of hosts actually fly by the seat of their pants, especially during a solo episode. It's almost like stream of consciousness, sometimes, and I'm always surprised by the bits of gold that can come from that. Sure, you have to do some research when you have a guest, so you'll be able to speak knowledgeably to them, but even then, the best conversations come from the spontaneous questions.

What's the biggest hack you've learned that you wish you could tell your younger podcasting self?

The biggest hack is actually something one of my coaches taught me about interviewing: Don't write down a bunch of questions to fire at your guest. Instead, just put these three questions on the desk in front of you and ask them one at a time, about whatever your guest has just said:

WHY (did you do that),

HOW (did that happen/did that work), &

WHAT (did you do next/would you suggest...)

THE COMMUNITY SAFETY PODCAST

Name: Jim Nixon

Time as a podcaster: 12 months

Show: The Community Safety Podcast

'Transforming Communities and Saving Lives'

What do you wish you knew before starting podcasting?

Just how much hard work it is to get your shows out and the main advice I would give is to outsource as much as you can if you can afford it. There are some inexpensive options out there. Who wants to be editing at 3am in the morning to meet a show deadline. Try and be the talent and leave the rest to the experts.

What's the biggest hack you've learned that you wish you could tell your younger podcasting self?

Know your avatar audience and specifically target them and target them consistently. Don't get pulled into the trap that you will reach everyone. It's simply not true and you will soon be disheartened.

HOW TO DIE HAPPY

Name: Martin O'Toole

Time as a podcaster: Two months

Show: How To Die Happy

'Stories & practical utilities for the arts of living and dying well.'

What do you wish you knew before starting podcasting?

Hands down, I wish I knew about all-in-one digital podcast mixers! Following poor advice, I blew a lot of cash on an audio interface, then on a 12-channel mixer, plus iPad and soundboard software. Shortly afterwards, I discovered the Tascam Mixmaster 4 and my whole world changed! Of course, there are others (the Roder Caster, for example), but honestly, check them out as they're an all-in-one podcast production unit for the not-so-technically minded.

What's the biggest hack you've learned that you wish you could tell your younger podcasting self?

My hack would have to be mastering Adobe Audition. It takes a little learning. I had a crash course two days after my producer threw everything up in the air and left without notice. But being able to create a podcast from my head to your headphones using pro tech? Man oh man, it makes editing and mixing an absolute joy.

COME ON MAN - A 3% MAN PODCAST

Name: Paul Bauer

Time as a podcaster: A little over a year

Show: Come On Man - A 3% Man Podcast

A podcast for fellow students of Corey Wayne's book, "How To Be a 3% Man" and for men who just want to be better in general.

What do you wish you knew before starting podcasting?

My first attempt at podcasting was several years ago, and I ended up giving up on it because it became a daunting task. I was attempting a weekly political show, and what made it difficult was having to stay up to date with all of the current events. It became a full-time job for something that I just wanted to do for fun. That made it not very fun.

What I ended up figuring out was that it's better to find a format that doesn't require current events. That way you can record a number of episodes in advance, and put them in the proverbial can to be scheduled out later. It allows you to take breaks when you need to and keeps everything fun. The way it should be.

My current format is a self-improvement based podcast for men. This allows me to interview guests, and review books on my time. I am having so much more fun with this podcast than any of my other previous attempts.

What's the biggest hack you've learned that you wish you could tell your younger podcasting self?

The biggest hack I found was to utilize TikTok to leverage the fast audience growth that it offers. Once

I started promoting my podcast on TikTok, it really took off. The sad thing about this question is that I couldn't tell my younger self that because TikTok didn't exist back then. If you are just getting started though, it does exist now, so use it!

PENCIL LEADERSHIP PODCAST

Name: Chris Anderson

Time as a podcaster: Since 2019

Show: Pencil Leadership Podcast

'Leave your positive mark on the world.'

What do you wish you knew before starting podcasting?

My podcast is an extension of my business, so the one thing I wish I knew before starting is related to using it to grow my business.

I wish I could go back and tell my younger self to narrow down and be specific on your target audience member. Growth comes a lot simpler when you have a specific, dialled-in idea of to whom you're speaking. Because when you try to speak to everyone, you speak to no one.

When you know who you are speaking to, on an intimate level, the marketing of your show will be more streamlined and precise. Unless your podcast is just a labor of love, a hobby to use your time up, then you need to look at it as a business, even if you don't have anything to sell just yet.

There are so many avenues to monetize your show and create something that isn't just a money pit but something that can produce more money for you each month if that's what you want. You need to build it as though it's a business, and that is why narrowing down your niche with you who speak to is so crucial.

What's the biggest hack you've learned that you wish you could tell your younger podcasting self?

There are a lot of "hacks" that can make podcasting not as big of a chore as it could be. However, if I could only go back and tell my younger podcasting self one thing, it would have to be batch record as soon as possible. Because my podcast is my business, it was easier for me to select one day each month to record 4-6 new episodes of my show.

Batching episodes allowed me to edit and get everything prepped the following weekend and be done with it all for a whole month. Yes, it was tiring and draining during those days, but the day after each batch/block time slot, I would have the day off to recover.

Even if you can't take a whole day during the week off for recording, you might be able to batch on the first Saturday of each month and sacrifice that one weekend. Then edit the following Saturday. It takes the sacrifice of some comfort to have success. But batching episodes freed up a lot more time by focusing on one thing, recording, editing, or publishing, on a specific day.

So, batching your recording, editing, and publishing tasks on their days and focusing only on those things during those days. So that's three days, maybe five, each month that you're dedicating to the technical aspect of podcasting and then rest you can use to market, find guests, or just enjoy your hard work.

#BEINGAFRICAALLAH

Name: Africa Allah

Time as a podcaster: 16 years

Show: #beingAfricaAllah

'Culture. Music. Conversation'

What do you wish you knew before starting podcasting?

We started with the rise of podcasting and grew with the industry. I wish we had the foresight to start monetizing earlier.

What's the biggest hack you've learned that you wish you could tell your younger podcasting self?

Conversation translates better than interviews.

Printed in Great Britain
by Amazon

39602441R00116